Fire Fighters

By Robert Maass

SCHOLASTIC
HARDCOVER

SCHOLASTIC INC. / New York

Library of Congress Cataloging-in-Publication Data
Maass, Robert.
Fire Fighters
Summary: Describes what it means to be a fire fighter,
including life at the firehouse, practice drills, service
to the community, and fire emergencies. 1. Fire fighters—
Juvenile literature. 2. Fire extinction—Juvenile literature.
[1. Fire fighters. 2. Occupations] I. Title.
TH 9148.M24 1989   628.9'2   88-18340
ISBN 0-590-41459-3

12 11 10 9 8 7 6 5 4 3 2 1   9/8 0 1 2 3 4/9

Printed in the U.S.A.   36
First Scholastic printing, May 1989

Unlimited thanks and appreciation go to
the fire fighters depicted in this book, who generously
gave their time and cooperation. Particular thanks are owed
to Lt. Frank Martinez of the New York City Fire Dept.,
whose cooperation and good humor helped tremendously.
And finally thanks to Brenda Bowen, Craig Walker,
and Claire Counihan whose encouragement
and enthusiasm made it all happen.

What do fire fighters do?

They have many different jobs. Their most important job is fighting fires to save lives and property. They learn this job by going to school. They are taught by experienced fire fighters.

To be a fire fighter, one of the first things to learn is how to use ladders for climbing.

Fire fighters also learn how to use ropes. They use ropes the way mountain climbers do. With a rope, fire fighters can lower themselves down a wall.

Fire fighters in training learn all about the hoses they use to fight fires. They must practice the correct way to aim the nozzle. A fire hose shoots out water with great force. It takes skill to make sure the water goes where it is supposed to go.

The hoses are attached to fire hydrants and then to the *pumper truck*. The pumper truck pumps the water from the hydrants into the hoses the fire fighters use. These hoses are called *lines*. Controlling the amount of water that comes out of the lines is an important job. Fire fighters must learn to read the gauges on the pumper truck to know when to pump more or less water into the lines. It is a job that takes lots of practice.

There are many special tools the fire fighters must learn to use. One of these tools is called the "jaws of life." It is a very powerful tool that can cut through metal. It can also be used to pry things open. When people are stuck in cars or buildings, this tool can help get them out.

There are also simple tools a fire fighter needs. One of the most important is an ax. Fire fighters often need it to break through walls, ceilings, doors, and windows during a fire.

All fire fighters wear heavy coats and gloves when fighting fires. They also wear an unusual leather helmet. It protects them from water and from things that might fall from burning buildings.

A flashlight and a doorstop come in very handy, too. They are used so often that fire fighters sometimes carry them on their helmets.

Fire fighters also wear special gear. They need to wear walkie-talkies to stay in touch with one another. They wear heat-resistant clothing because the fire is very hot. Often a fire fighter must carry a tank of air to breathe when there is a lot of smoke.

Some fire fighters receive special training. They may be assigned to a *rescue unit.* The fire fighters in these units fight fires, but also need special skills. For example, some are trained in diving to fight ship or pier fires. Diving rescue units may also be called to help people who have boating or other water accidents.

Teamwork is a very important part of learning to be a fire fighter. Everyone must work together to save lives and put out fires. Fire fighters at school march together to practice being part of a team.

After several weeks the fire fighters' basic training is over. All fire fighters must pass a test on what they have learned. Then the fire fighters graduate.

The new graduates are assigned to work with experienced fire fighters at a fire station.

Here they will put their training into practice, and learn even more from the experienced fire fighters. There are many new jobs to learn at the fire station.

All of the equipment the fire fighters use must be kept in top shape. This means that repairs must be done as soon as anything goes wrong. New fire fighters learn to maintain and repair their equipment. Tools and trucks are checked and serviced every day, because everything must work perfectly when a fire or other emergency happens.

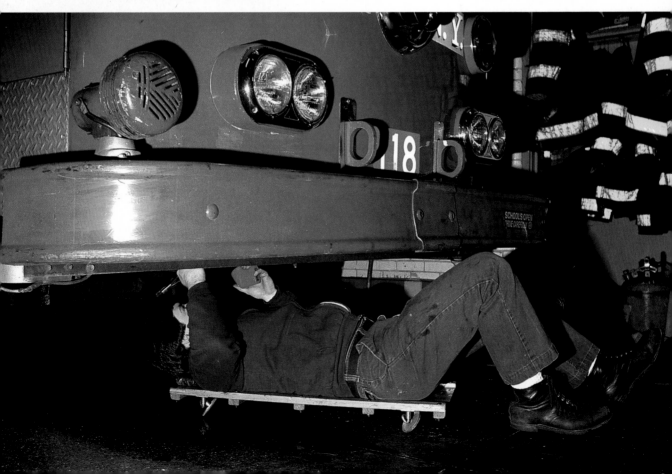

Fire fighters must also learn to check things outside of the fire station. They check all of the fire hydrants in the neighborhoods they serve, and inspect buildings for fire safety.

There are lots of other jobs around the fire station.

Fires can break out at any time, so fire fighters in many places must be at the fire station every day and every night. That means that the fire fighters on duty must cook their own meals.

When they go shopping for groceries, they must all go together. They take their walkie-talkies to keep in touch. If a fire starts some-where, the fire fighters will have to leave the grocery store in a hurry.

There are often visitors at the fire station. School children sometimes come to learn about fire fighting and fire prevention.

When children can't come to the fire station, fire fighters visit schools. They talk to classes about fire prevention, and what to do in case of fire.

Fire fighters demonstrate how to *stop-drop-and-roll.* This is what you must do if your clothes catch on fire. **Stop:** Stop where you are. Don't run. **Drop:** Drop to the ground. **Roll:** Roll back and forth protecting your face with your hands to smother the flames.

When all of the work has been done at the fire station, there are other things to do. Some fire fighters may get a chance to read the paper. Some may exercise in order to keep in shape. There may be a dog to take care of, too.

Occasionally, fire fighters may even try to sleep. But no matter what fire fighters may be doing, they must always be ready. Because sooner or later, usually when no one is expecting it...the alarm will ring.

As soon as the alarm goes off, the fire fighters must put on their fire-fighting gear and get to their trucks as fast as they can. Many fire stations have poles to help fire fighters get downstairs. Poles are faster and safer than stairs. Everyone hurries. They know that the best way to control a fire is to get there as quickly as possible.

Each fire fighter has a special place on one of the trucks. As the engines pull out of the fire station, the fire fighters check the equipment they will need.

Some of the trucks need two drivers. One is in the front of the truck and one is at the back, or *tiller*. The one in the back handles the rear wheels of the longest fire trucks.

As soon as they arrive, the fire fighters jump off the trucks and go to work. Each fire fighter knows what to do.

A fire chief is on hand to direct the firefight.

Some of the fire fighters must *vent* the roof. That means they must break a hole in the roof to release fire and smoke trapped in the building. That will make it easier to fight the fire and rescue people inside.

Other fire fighters have attached the lines to pumper trucks. They begin to aim streams of water at the flames. Some must enter the building to fight the fire from inside.

Windows must sometimes be broken to let the smoke and heat out of the building. Fire fighters carry tanks of air on their backs so they can breathe pure air when the smoke is very thick.

The flames and smoke of the fire begin to disappear as the fire fighters gain control of it. After a while, the fire appears to be over. But the fire fighters' job is not over. They must carefully check the building to make sure that every bit of the fire is out.

Finally, the fire is completely out.

Struggling to put out a fire is exhausting work. Some of the fire fighters must rest before they put their equipment back into the trucks.

The fire-fighting team packs all of its tools and gear back into the trucks. Everything will be ready when the next fire occurs. The fire trucks return to the fire station. They back in so they will be ready to roll as soon as the alarm sounds again.

The fire fighters are happy to be back at the fire station. They are tired, but they are safe.

Fire fighting is very dangerous work. Sometimes fire fighters lose their lives in fires.

But the brave men and women who have died fighting fires are not forgotten. In almost every city and town, there is a monument to remember those who gave their lives trying to save others. At least once each year, fire fighters get together to remember.

In many places fire fighters also get together to take part in special parades. Fire fighters wash and shine all of their trucks so they will look their very best on parade day. Then they get dressed in fresh uniforms.

Fire fighters love marching in parades with music and flags.

So do future fire fighters.